T0039715

Nico Muhly

PASTORAL

for Piano

Commissioned by Planting Fields Foundation,

Oyster Bay, New York

St Rose Music Publishing Co.
/ Chester Music Ltd.

for Conor Hanick, and Planting Fields

PASTORAL

NICO MUHLY

I. Aubade

♩ = 86 – 92, flexible

Copyright © 2021 by St Rose Music Publishing Co. and Chester Music Limited.

II. Calls

Pressing slightly

sim., B's softer, *più lontano*

*B's always quieter than other notes; accented and *marcatissimo* notes always outside of the dynamic

III. Chorale